3 1994 01289 6970

D1505757

MILITARY VEHICLES

U.S.

ARMY

HUMVEES

by Angie Peterson Kaelberer

Reading Consultant:
Barbara J. Fox
Reading Specialist
North Carolina State University

Capstone

Mankato, Minnesota

Blazers is published by Capstone Press,
151 Good Counsel Drive, P.O. Box 669, Mankato, Minnesota 56002.
www.capstonepress.com

Library of Congress Cataloging-in-Publication Data
Kaelberer, Angie Peterson.
    U.S. Army Humvees / by Angie Peterson Kaelberer.
    p. cm.—(Blazers. Military vehicles)
    Summary: "Describes Humvees, their design, weapons, and role in the U.S.
Army"—Provided by publisher.
    Includes bibliographical references and index.
    ISBN-13: 978-0-7368-6458-9 (hardcover)
    ISBN-10: 0-7368-6458-X (hardcover)
    1. Hummer trucks. 2. United States—Armed Forces—Transportation—
History—20th century. I. Title. II. Series.
    UG618.K34 2007
    623.7'4722—dc22   2006002542

Editorial Credits
Martha E. H. Rustad, editor; Thomas Emery, set designer; Ted Williams, book
    designer; Jo Miller, photo researcher/photo editor

Photo Credits
AM General Corporation, LLC/Rob Wurtz, 7 (bottom), 8–9, 11 (bottom), 13,
    18–19
AP/Wide World Photos/Antonio Castaneda, 12; Khalid Mohammed, 7 (top)
Check Six/Dan Snellgroves, 24–25; John Clark, 15; Sam Sargent, 11 (top),
    22–23, 28–29
Corbis/Peter Turnley, 26–27 (bottom)
DVIC/SPC Patrick Tharpe, 14
Getty Images Inc./Joseph Giordono, 4–5; Mario Tama, 26–27 (top); Robert
    Nickelsberg, 20–21; Scott Nelson, cover; U.S. Marines/Gordon A. Rouse,
    16–17

**Capstone Press thanks Craig C. Mac Nab, Director of Public Relations for
    AM General LLC, for his assistance with this book.**

TABLE OF CONTENTS

HUMVEES

A line of huge vehicles barrels over bumpy desert roads. Heavy armor protects the U.S. Army soldiers inside. The vehicles are Humvees.

Humvees work hard for the U.S. military. Some Humvees bring soldiers to missions. Others launch weapons. Some Humvees carry hurt soldiers to hospitals.

BLAZER FACT

The Humvee's full name is High Mobility Multipurpose Wheeled Vehicle.

DESIGN

Humvees are long, wide,
and powerful. They are high
above the ground so they can
drive over tall objects.

Even though Humvees are large and heavy, they move quickly. Their top speed is 78 miles (126 kilometers) per hour.

Humvees rumble easily over rough ground. They climb steep hills. Not even deep water stops a Humvee.

BLAZER FACT

Humvees use special equipment to travel through water up to 5 feet (1.5 meters) deep.

13

BLAZER FACT

CH-47 Chinook helicopters can carry two Humvees at the same time.

Helicopters and planes carry Humvees to faraway missions. Humvees hang from helicopters as they are lowered to the ground.

★ ★ ★ ★ ★ ★

15

WEAPONS AND EQUIPMENT

Humvees carrying weapons on their turrets are a threat to enemies. Powerful missiles and machine guns can blow up targets in a flash.

TURRET

17

Humvees have run-flat tires. Even if all four tires go flat, the Humvee can still go another 30 miles (48 kilometers).

Humvees with metal armor on the sides and underbody are called up-armored Humvees. This tough armor protects the soldiers inside from many enemy weapons.

BLAZER FACT

Up-armored Humvees weigh 9,800 pounds (4,500 kilograms).

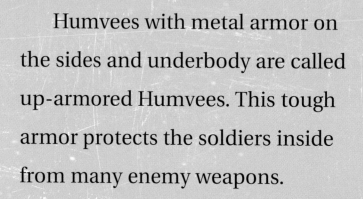

HUMVEE DIAGRAM

ARMOR

RUN-FLAT TIRE

MACHINE GUN

TURRET

23

HUMVEES ON DUTY

About 10 soldiers and their gear can fit in the back of a Humvee. Some Humvees carry extra cargo in the back.

25

★ ★ ★ ★ ★ ★

Humvees carry soldiers, weapons, and supplies all over the world. They can handle any kind of weather and all types of land. They help keep the military on the move.

BLAZER FACT

General Motors sells a nonmilitary version of the Humvee called a Hummer.

27

READY TO FIGHT!

GLOSSARY

armor (AR-mur)—a protective covering made of metal or ceramic materials

cargo (KAR-goh)—objects carried by a ship, aircraft, or other vehicle

missile (MISS-uhl)—a weapon that flies and blows up when it hits a target

mission (MISH-uhn)—a military task

run-flat tire (RUHN-FLAT TIRE)—an inflated tire with a hard plastic center that allows the vehicle to move even if the wheel is punctured

target (TAR-git)—something that is aimed at or shot at

turret (TUR-it)—a rotating structure on top of a military vehicle that holds a weapon

READ MORE

Green, Michael. *Humvee at War.* At War. St. Paul, Minn.: Zenith Press, 2005.

Healy, Nick. *High Mobility Vehicles: The Humvees.* War Machines. Mankato, Minn.: Capstone Press, 2005.

Piehl, Janet. *Humvees.* Pull Ahead Books. Minneapolis: Lerner, 2006.

INTERNET SITES

FactHound offers a safe, fun way to find Internet sites related to this book. All of the sites on FactHound have been researched by our staff.

Here's how:
1. Visit *www.facthound.com*
2. Choose your grade level.
3. Type in this book ID **073686458X** for age-appropriate sites. You may also browse subjects by clicking on letters, or by clicking on pictures and words.
4. Click on the **Fetch It** button.

FactHound will fetch the best sites for you!

INDEX

armor, 4, 20

cargo, 24

enemies, 16, 20

helicopters, 14, 15
Hummers, 27

missions, 6, 15

run-flat tires, 19

soldiers, 4, 6, 20, 24, 27
speed, 10

turrets, 16

up-armored
    Humvees, 20

weapons, 6, 16, 20, 27
    machine guns, 16
    missiles, 16